Language Buddies;
A Program for Supporting Language and Literacy in Schools

All Rights Reserved
No reproduction by any means
except for purchaser's own class

Copyright, Mainstreams Publications
ISBN 0-9731493-3-7

Table of Contents

1	Introduction
2	Just Imagine
4	Background
5	What are Language Buddies?
7	Research Says
8	Language Learning is a Process
11	Talk Activities are Noisy
12	What Kinds of Activities?
13	How is an Activity Prescriptive?
14	Sample Paper Based Activities
15	Items for Language Activities
16	Resources on Hand
17	Resources to Acquire
18	What Happens with Language Buddies?
19	Where Do I Start?
20	Who Trains My Buddies?
21	Supportive Talk
22	Tips for Buddies
23	A Buddy Contract
24	Getting Language Buddies Going
25	Inclusion Activities
26	Planning and Tracking Sheet
28	Matching Activities to Needs
30	Language Buddies Grades 7-12
31	Cooperative Learning
32	Knowing What To Do
34	Talk on Task Content, Planning
35	Content Form, Key Vocabulary and Summary
36	A Beginner's Program
37	Why Use Bingo?
38	What's Missing? Game
39	Reproducible Ideas for Buddy Work

Isn't this wonderful! It really sounds like learning.

Language Buddies;
Supporting Language and Literacy in Schools

Introduction

A superintendent once asked me to envision what I would want to see happen for ESL programs in an ideal world. I can't remember why some important fellow would come out to see me, but here he was, and there I was, with the undivided attention of an erudite educator. I looked skyward, and naively rattled on about ideas and plans for services. I never heard anything after that, and my 'in the best of all worlds' suggestions came to naught. I would like you, however, to keep the essence of that question in mind while reading the following pages.

As an elementary school teacher I loved working with kids face-to-face and collaborating with great colleagues. These offered me lively challenges, but I became equally fascinated with my own learning. I learned that a grade's curriculum didn't always match a student's readiness, and that every human being needs acceptance and success in order to want to learn further. The diversity of the communities I worked in taught me more about life than any lecture or book. The longer I taught, the more often I stood looking into classrooms in awe, recognizing and appreciating the complexity of a teacher's job well done.

I want to share my favorite memory. Once, a little fellow, maybe grade 5 or so came walking into my ESL room. He was late as usual, but that was a good sign; he was becoming more and more comfortable with his own classroom work and he wanted to stay there longer. Anyway, in through the open door he sauntered, books tucked under his arm, and he remarked matter-of-factly, "Why do they call this the ESL room? Why don't they call it the laughing room?" Language Buddies epitomizes that feeling for me.

'Language Buddies' represents the culmination of over 30 years of teaching, observation, research, reflection, practice, and dialogue with colleagues. I'm thrilled to share with you what the kids and others have taught me. Most of all, I wish you laughter.

Just Imagine!

Imagine working in a school with a stated priority to support and guide both teachers and students with the successful integration of exceptional students.

Visualize this commitment accompanied by an administrative purchase of resources games and professional materials.

Let's say that these resources, activities, and games would address student needs in different areas; ESL levels, readiness, remediation and skills learning.

What if all of those materials could be used and copied by all teachers - no matter what their grade or role?

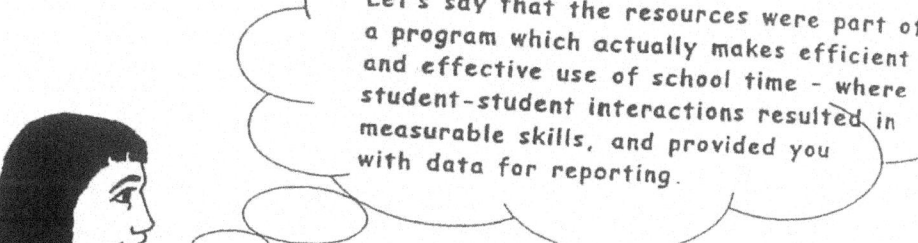

> Let's say that the resources were part of a program which actually makes efficient and effective use of school time - where student-student interactions resulted in measurable skills, and provided you with data for reporting.

> Imagine using the guides and resources in this program to fulfill requirements for professional development in TESL, Teaching English as a Second Language.

> What if teachers could choose where and how they wanted to opt in to the program?

> Imagine if your strengths, creativity, leadership, and collegiality in the program were applauded?

Background

Policy for Equity in education has been in place for many years, yet the reality of teacher training, staffing, resources, and in-school learning opportunities to address the needs in multiethnic schools, has been fraught with setbacks and problems. Thurgood Marshall stated, 'There is nothing so unequal as the equal treatment of unequals', and educators do daily battle with this dilemma, trying to meet the promise of equality for the diversity of students in our schools.

'Language Buddies' is an offshoot of research I began in the '80s to develop an effective and viable approach for the provision of language supports within regular classrooms. In Great Britain, research and inquiry led policy makers there to support a whole-school approach to plan for and improve language teaching and learning. Such an approach shares the burden of responsibility for language supports between both administrators and teachers. I see Language Buddies as one aspect of a school-wide approach. I believe that this program can assist teachers with incorporating effective second language strategies, and can offer linguistically disadvantaged students more effective learning supports.

The framework for a school-based approach is three-fold:
- an administrative priority on long-term leadership and support for this endeavor
- teacher access to a wide variety of suitable ESL resources, interactive language activities and games to be used with the Language Buddies program and finally,
- professional development for staff in the field of TESL.

It was clear that Language Buddies could be implemented for ESL students and non-ESL students alike. Indeed, if Language Buddies were incorporated across all grades, ESL students would then be supported over a longer period of time, and especially with the language challenges in higher grades.

This guide explains the basic concepts of 'Language Buddies', how to get started, and how teachers can use the program to prescribe specific remediation for student needs. At the very least, Language Buddies will act as a springboard to challenge traditional teaching styles in multi-lingual classrooms.

What are Language Buddies?

Language Buddies builds on the basic premise that student pair interactions provide positive experiences for both individuals. Most schools are familiar with pairing an older student with a younger child as a reading buddy. Although pleasurable, being read to is a receptive skill only, that of listening. Without question-answer interactions and re-readings of the same story, language learners miss opportunities to develop fluency, and extend comprehension.

Language Buddies should be viewed as a legitimate learning activity and part of the regular school day; not a frill, or an add-on since the program actually addresses student needs in language, skills development, and curriculum remediation.

The Language Buddies program adds wings.

"Language codes the experience you are having."
Gordon Wells in 'The Meaning Makers'

> With Language Buddies
> there is a change in dynamics.
> Both buddy and learner see progress.

The dynamics of a good language buddy grouping
is such that the older buddy and each student
can actually see progress.

It is so encouraging to the older buddy to be able
to actually see the changes in his/her charges;
to know the effects of his/her interactions.

This growth in confidence and self-esteem for both
the buddy and his/her students will embolden them.
Success breeds success; and in essence
that's the best of all worlds.

What Happens With Language Buddies?

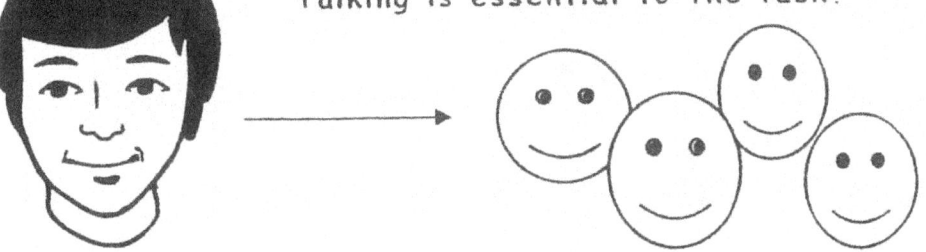

A buddy leads a group through an activity. Talking is essential to the task.

ESL students improve their fluency using "talk" activities.

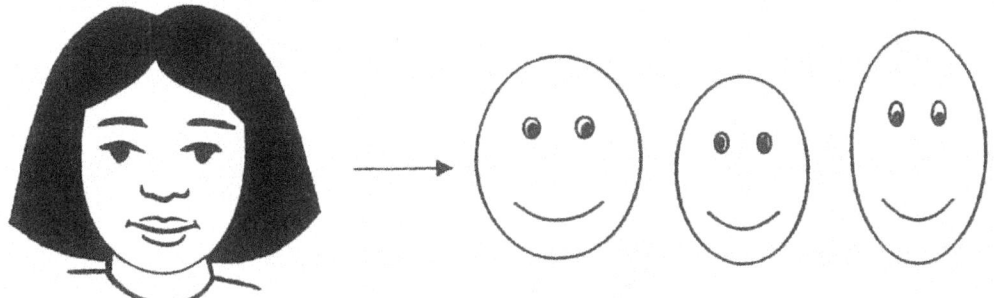

The more vocabulary students learn, the more language they have to comprehend new ideas and skills.

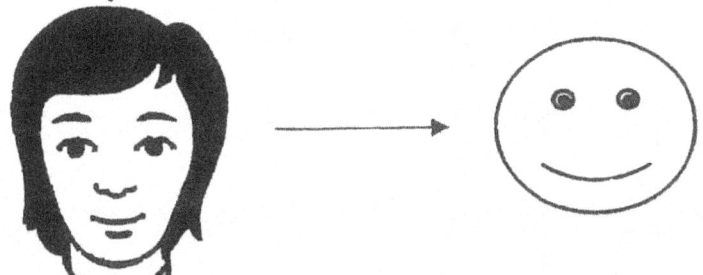

Special needs and remedial students are supported by the verbal guidance and leadership of a language buddy. Work becomes easier, success becomes the norm and students grow in confidence.

You may want to group your class by language, remediation or skills needs. It is up to you to arrange for as many, or as few, buddies as you feel are right for you.

Teachers Choose the Activity

Teachers can choose any activity for Buddy time and they can choose different activities for different groups. Teachers control the content of practise and review activities.

Subject-specific curriculum support can be provided by buddy activities:

* re-reading and talking about a section
* talking students through a practise test
* a session on new vocabulary and translations
* assistance with summarizing or note-taking
* a session on 'what I know & what I don't know'
* help students with locating data via skimming
* conduct an 'Explanation Session'. The students explain a topic or main events to the Buddy or provide reasons and opinions on a topic, etc. Teachers write the exact activity on a card.

How is an Activity Prescriptive?

> An activity becomes prescriptive when a teacher uses it to specifically address a student's needs in language or literacy.

> A teacher can prescribe activities as learning supports for students. For example, a teacher could prescribe a once a week Language Buddy activity to support certain students in spelling, while other groups are assigned activities to promote fluency, vocabulary, editing and conferencing, missed skills, etc.

> Teachers can move students across groups according to their changing needs.

> Teachers can plan a different focus for different days. One weekly session could be content-oriented and the next session might focus on vocabulary or fluency.

Language Buddies

- improve the learning of language skills for ESL students as well as for non-ESL students

- incorporate a broad range of activities and games to support and build language acquisition in many contexts

- add a focus on vocabulary building, oral fluency, literacy remediation and enrichment

- address student needs in language, literacy skills and curriculum review, and as such are integral to, not superfluous to day to day teaching activities

- extend the scope and type of supports for students

- allow teachers to prescribe specific learning activities

- provide resources and activities more appropriate for students learning English in addition to their home language

- promote relationships across linguistic, cultural and institutional differences (between schools and communities)

- infuse a school with ESL strategies, as teachers incorporate new knowledge, methodologies and ideas

- assure Equity in school plans and practices by gearing specific, long-term, and professional supports for ESL

- increase students' involvement in their own learning through comfortable interaction

- support teachers with professional development materials

"In Our Classrooms: An Educator's Guide to Helping English Language Learners With Curriculum" and *"Teaching to Diversity: Teaching and Learning in the Multiethnic Classroom"* are two very accessible and practical professional texts.

Research Says

ESL Students	Language Buddies' Effect
* Need a foundation of basic skills	√
* Need to learn basic vocabulary/ fill in gaps	√
* Need warm, positive, verbal interactions	√
* Need interactive practice and verbal review	√
* Need to use lots of visuals and manipulatives	√
* Need 'comprehensible' input	√
* Need to feel included, and free to take risks	√
* Need language skills taught at their levels	√
* Need to interact with native English speakers	√
* Need to verbalize often in collaborative settings	√
* Need to link oral language to literacy skills	√
* Need to see and hear progress	√
* Need to be assessed from their starting point	√

Inclusion means involvement

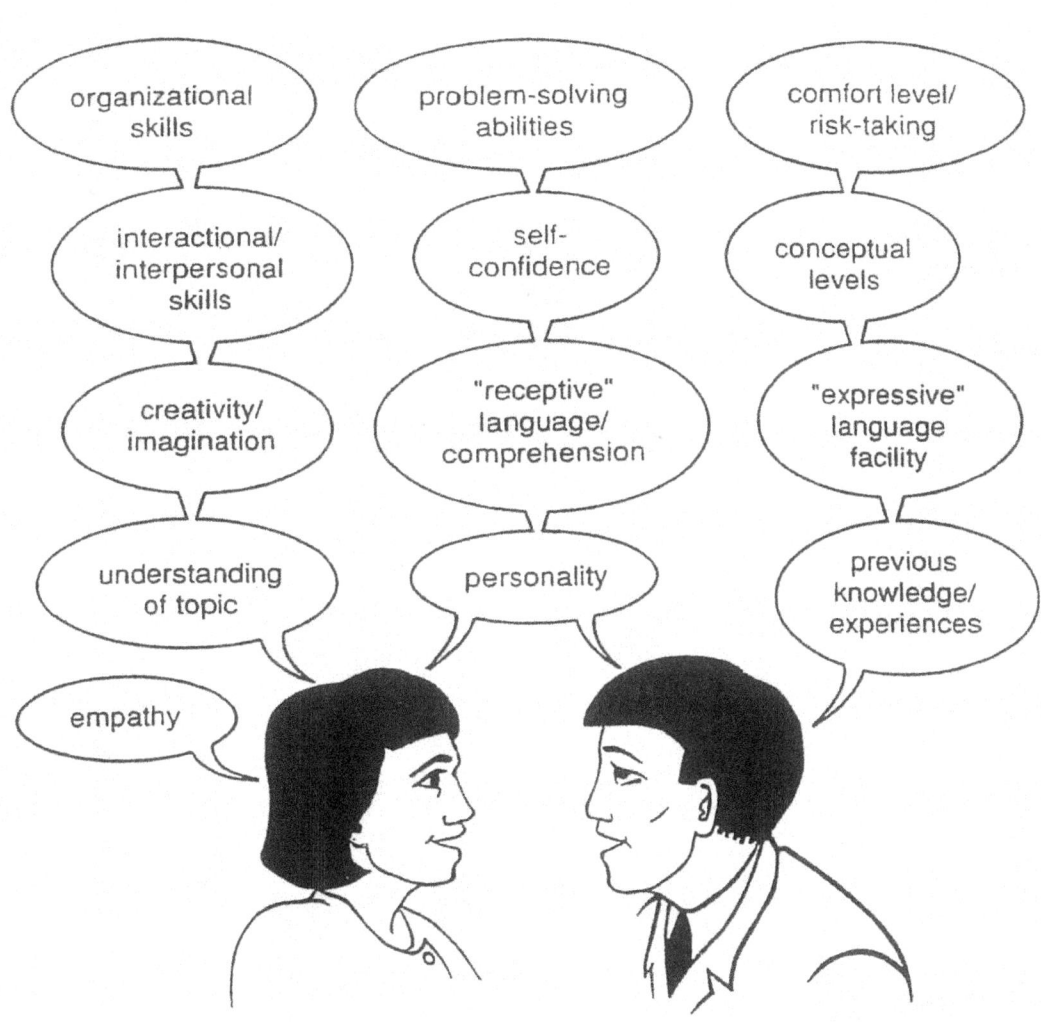

What Kinds of Activities Are Involved?

arts and crafts

bingo games   literacy

board games

science

skill building games

vocabulary games

matching, sequencing, planning activities

sports games

tutorials

mapping

maths

library skills

camera activities   making booklets

following directions

skills cut and paste

video production

library skills

drama   research

directed play

letter writing

remediation

genre

use of graphic organizers

varied reading sources

computer work

"Talk" Activities are Noisy

- Language Buddies is a learning time not simply play time.

- Expect excitement and laughter. But, you can lower the noise by using other spaces; halls, lobby, even the library - with supervision.

- Agree on a signal for "too noisy" and "time to stop", perhaps flicking the lights off.

- Learning a language, and trying to keep up with the class as new language and literacy skills are taught is a challenge. The same is true for special needs students. When we can pace and present information in different and interesting ways, students will be more receptive, and learning will be more effective.

- Timing is crucial. Plan 35 to 45 minute time blocks for Language Buddies. Account for settling in, activity time and cleanup. Too short a time may frustrate the groups.

- Certain activities may run two sessions or more.

- Before lunch or home time are best for doing Language Buddies. Keep key learning times in the first part of the morning and afternoon for teacher instruction.

It's a good idea to have 'helpers' who will clean up.

Sample Paper-based Activities

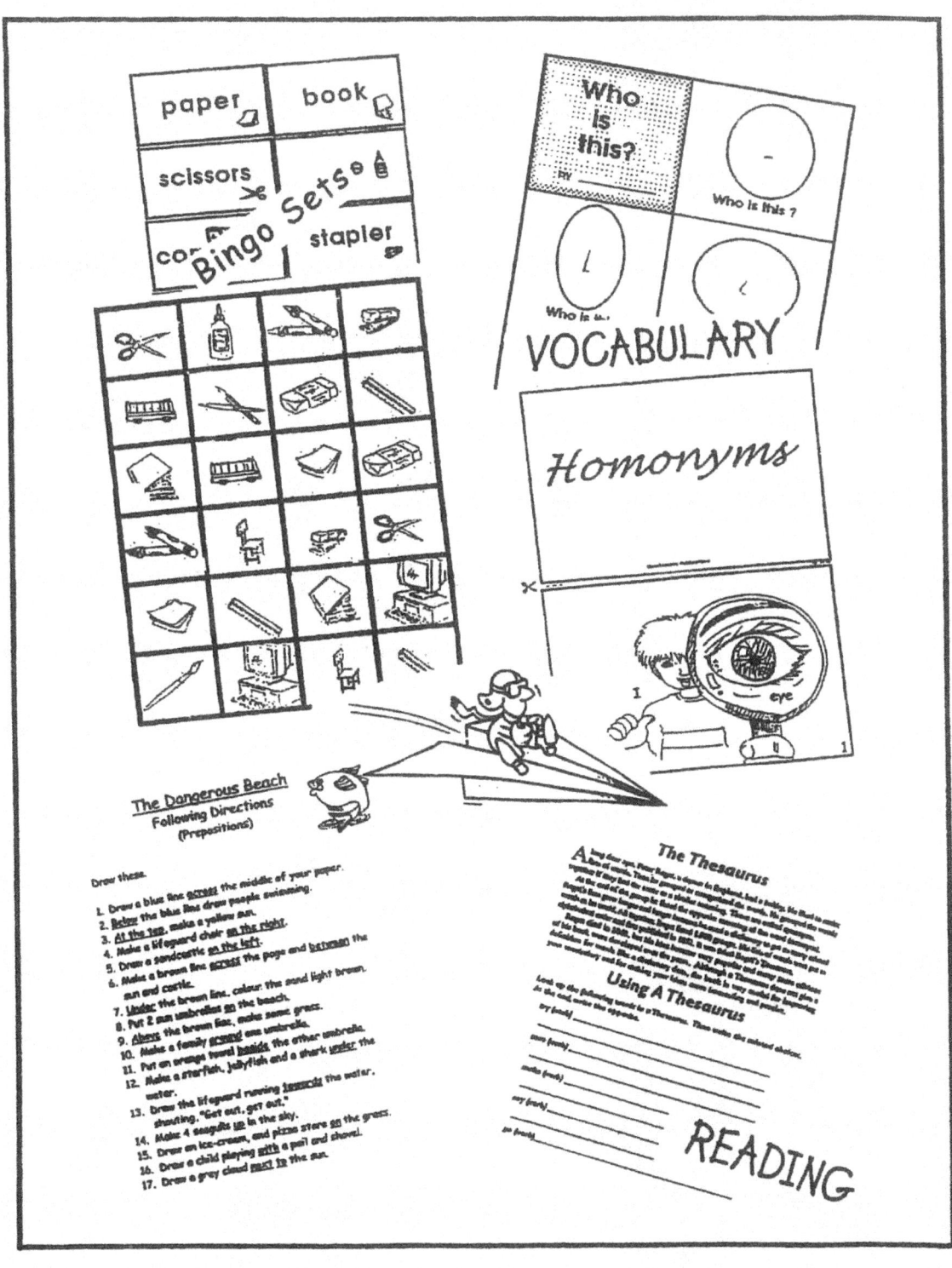

Items for Language-based Activities

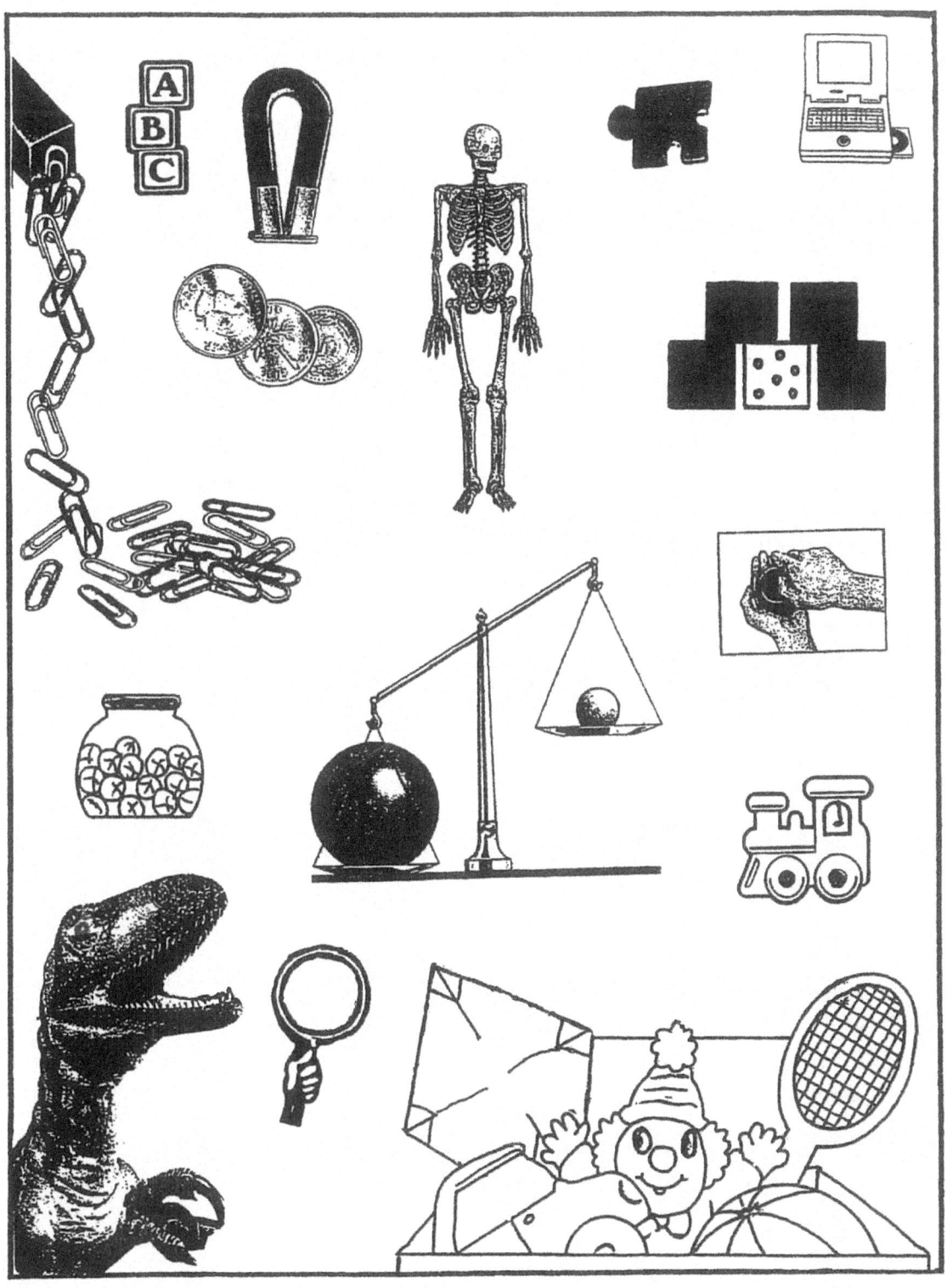

Resources On Hand

Instructional Leaders in Arts, Music and main subject areas can be guest specialists and/or speakers, as well as offer ideas and materials for language activities in their area of expertise.

Arts and Crafts references

Book-binding machine/spiral binder

Sports Equipment

Math Base ten stamp set, geometry stamps

Science Magnifying Glasses Magnets
Microscopes Models
Scales Magic Ideas

Toys
- plastic animals
- different sizes and categories of puzzles
- buildings – farm, house, hospital, zoo etc.
- different sizes and types of building blocks
- sand and water tables and equipment
- Drama Props, Puppet Theatre and puppets

Shared, Graded Skill Activities
- compound word matching games
- Dolch High Frequency Word Bingo
- Sequence Story Cards
- Manipulative Letters, etc.

Board Games with a Focus on Speaking
- Guess Who? questioning (is it a __? Does she have __?)
- Monopoly – money, requests
-
-

Camera and Video-cam

Resources To Acquire

The Card Book; ESL Games, ISBN 0-13-115767-1
Prentice Hall Inc.
Games for Language Learning, ISBN 0-521-27737-X

Place Value Stamps
Money Stamps
Alphabet Stamps

Dolch High Frequency Words Bingo

Scholastic Book Co., Joke Books, Magic Books
Chickadee Publications, Dr. Zed's Science Surprises
Children's Magazines, Owl, Junior National Geographic

Card Sets; Compound Words, Rhyming Words, Money Match

- Bingos, 6 Topics – School, 2 Verbs, Locations, Clothing, Body

- Matching Pairs Card Games, Different Topics Pictures
- Both from Mainstreams Publications, FAX 416/698-8808

Where Do I Start?

Lay the Groundwork
- Everybody brings resources, games, and materials to a central location
- Decide which resources still need to be ordered
- Call subject area personnel for their ideas and supplies
- Decide where and how the resources will be accessed

Next plan a special day when staff can prepare all their activities, copy/enlarge/laminate paper resources, sign out library materials and then arrange their students into buddy groups

Then, approach a colleague(s) about using buddies from his/her class. Use the buddy "contract" sheet. Best days? Best time? Establish your groups and use the planning and tracking form as needed/desired. Plan a trip together

Fill the group tubs with talk activities. You can sequence items with sticky notes. Meet buddies

Getting Language Buddies Going

For Students	For Teachers

Sessions 1 and 2
* Inclusion Activities   * Set expectations for 'talk'

Create a sense of bonding and inclusion.
This will enhance involvement in future activities.
It is imperative to assure students that 'talking' is O.K.
and that talk is expected in certain learning situations.

Sessions 3 and 4
* Initial group interactions   * Observe and record
                                    - fluency behaviors
                                    - group dynamics

Students are placed in a buddy group for a fun activity. BINGO/craft
Encourage translation as needed, or even choose a bilingual buddy.
Record your initial observations of ESL students on a class list.
Tracking notes will allow you to gauge/comment on the ESL student's
growth in confidence, involvement, comprehension, fluency and skills.
Certain factors may require a 1-1 student interaction.
A good group should have no more than 4 students, and include 1 or 2
native English speakers to model language and learning tasks.

Thereafter
* Interactive tasks   * Assist group interactions
  (prescribed or not)   * Note readiness/needs
                                    for next language skill.

Choose an activity that lasts over several sessions. BINGOs/booklets
ESL and remedial students need repetition with new skills.
Teachers can match an activity to the need(s) of student(s). Groups
can be learning different skills/vocabulary/remediation. Teachers can
provide as much direction as they want. Even without prescribing and
sequencing skills, students will benefit from these interactions.

Inclusion Activities

Informal Visit
The buddies are introduced before a literacy task or craft activity, and then circulate around the class offering help as needed. Students become comfortable with each other, learn some names, and the buddies are viewed as support.

Meet The Experts
Students develop questions for the older buddies, and then are formally introduced to them. Buddies sit across the front and tell about themselves before they answer the students' questions. Be sure to insert a compliment or question for buddies who speak another language and can translate.

Names BINGO
The buddies' names are written on a blank BINGO form along with all the class names. Even your timid students will learn everybody's names.

Seasonal Trip
Hike a ravine or forested parkland with paths, bridges, fields. Allow students the freedom to explore and play as this will encourage talk, and encourage students to forge different relationships than they normally would back in the classroom.

Who Trains My Buddies?

All teachers should

- discuss 'Language Buddies' with their classes
- show and discuss some of the activities
- stress 'talking' as an important part of learning
- help buddies recognize supportive language

I need to

- meet with, and assign each buddy a group
- tell buddies about the members of that group
- have buddies look at the group's 'tub' activities
- take time to answer questions, and encourage buddies to come to you for direction or help
- restate the expectations for supportive talk
- address specific problems during/after sessions

Tips For Buddies

- Learn the names of students in your group.

- Talk clearly. Don't speak too fast.

- Repeat words, questions or directions if necessary. See who understands or doesn't. Let students translate for each other, or translate yourself if you can.

- Look directly at each student to get each child involved. Call them by name. Make a connection.

- If one student does all the talking, tell him/her in a nice way to give others a chance to speak.

- If a student is really shy and quiet, give them time. If that student doesn't start smiling and taking part in the activity eventually, inform the teacher.

- Have fun with the students.

- Praise the students. They will love that and you.

- You are kind, helpful and wonderful. Thank you.

Supportive Talk Sounds Like

It's alright! I'll help you.

Don't worry. Just watch me!

Let me help you.

We need to fix _____.

It's okay. Let's try again.

I'd like to hear from _____.

Can you help _____? Thank you.

I'll be your partner.

That's a great idea!

You're really getting better.

Good for you!

You remembered. Excellent!

Hey! That's great! Wow!

Between _____ & _____

Best Day(s) _____

_____

Time(s) _____

_____

Buddy Names

_____

_____

_____

* indicates a bilingual student/translator

Language Buddy Planner and Tracker
Group Names

Vocabulary	Skill Builders	Remediation
Bingos	Booklet-Making	Arts or Crafts
Science	Maths	Board Games
Performing Arts	Music – Movement	Guest Speakers Trip

Buddy   Date

Tracking Sheet

A planning and tracking sheet is useful for reporting purposes since the record of activities will demonstrate adaptations, remediation and interventions you have made for students. i.e., small group learning, specific skills addressed in vocabulary, fluency, upgrading and/or literacy skills, support for content learning.

Language Buddy Record

Group Names _____

Activity   Date

Language Observations

Student	Date & Notes

Sample Tubs	Matching Activities to Needs Primary Class
Group 1 3 times a week ALPHABET SKILLS	- Play matching pairs, small to capitals - Sequence alphabet manipulatives - Use computers to show font styles - Alphabet BINGO
Group 2 Four times a week SCHOOL VOCABULARY No English	- Play the 'What's Missing?' game - Make a school picture-word booklet - Play the game with new objects - Play school object BINGO - Let a student call the words
Group 3 3 times a week Color Words Literacy	- Make picture-word booklets - Spell colors with cut letters - Play 'What's missing with words - Re-read booklets
Group 4 3 times a week Fine motor skills Concrete to abstract	- Free choice with variety of puzzles - Beading with shoelaces - cutting shapes for headband - roll plasticene to cover letters - tracing activities
Group 5 3 times a week Enrichment/Review	- Play picture verb bingo (present tense) - Start to use past tense - A student gets to be verb caller - Choose one of these students to do bingo with ESL students another time

Sample Tubs

Matching Activities to Needs
Junior Class

Group 1
Twice a week
Syllable Skills

- Divide spelling words into syllables
- Clap out a list of multi-syllabic words
- List 2-3-4-5-6-7 syllable words
- Rules for double letters, single vowels
- Make a set of cards cut into syllables

Group 2
Four times a week
Past Tense Verbs
Basic English

- Play verb BINGO past tense
- Play the second verb BINGO set
- Let students call cards and sentences
- Cut out magazine pictures for verb words in the past tense, and make a class book.

Group 3
Twice a week
Abstract Nouns

- Continue a list of abstract nouns
- Find examples in magazines
- Make picture-word booklets
- Read each other's booklets

Group 4
Twice a week
Review letter wtg.
'I would appreciate...'

- share 'Free Stuff For Kid' books
- Show sample letter format
- Write letters for mailing
- Show form for addressing envelopes
- Write a 'request' to the principal
- Make up sentences for requesting something. i.e., Could you please, etc?

Group 5
Twice a week
Spelling Support

- Make up riddles for the week's words
- Say a sentence for the words
- Divide the words into syllables
- Play "Hangman"
- Pre-test and correct errors

Language Buddies
Grade 7-12

Cooperative Learning Replaces Language Buddies

Middle and high school curriculum demands and timetables do not suit Language Buddies.

Cooperative Learning activities support
- Students born here who speak another language
- Students who require remediation or support
- Students close to or at grade level
- Students who need extra motivation
- Racial harmony
- Skills learning

Learning Task	Skill Taught	Pair/Group Work
Text Info.	- recall - sequencing events	. movie frames . timelines
Novel Study	- understanding cause and effect - essay wtg	. graphic organizer . paired wtg
Essay writing etc.	- stating pro and con etc.	. graphic . expert gps . paired wtg

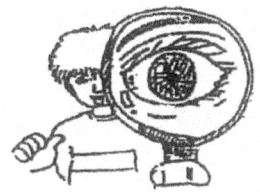

Language Buddies

Q. How does Language Buddies support students in Curriculum?

A. Teachers can set up the activities so that the older student guides a small group of students through a task that involves content knowledge and/or literacy learning.

Q. How can I simplify the process of instructing every student leader about what to do?

A. Prepare cards with content activities, and keep them from year to year. To review content, have the buddy lead ELLs through a homework activity or use a prior class task. In this way, ELLs are supported in a review of the content and of the language in that context. A leader could read parts of the text, practice pronunciation, or use one of the content games in this guide.

It is a good idea to have a selection of activities at different grade levels, even word games to practice word-building, plus science objects, board games, word bingos, etc.

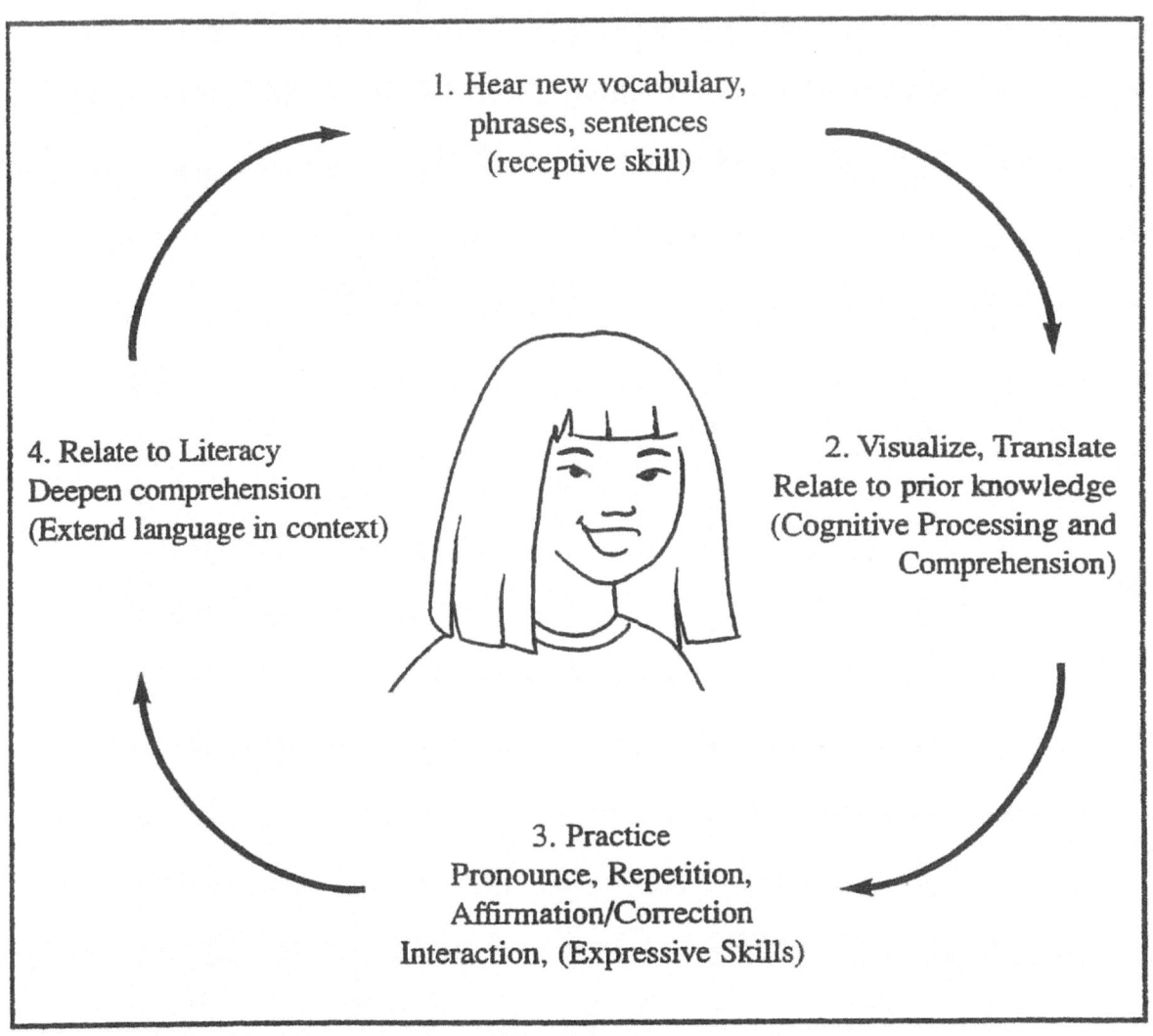

Focus on One

'Focus on One' is a strategy to bring a child into active participation. This technique works well for a student who is consistently and noticeably quiet and reserved, who is not actively engaged but is attentive. Using Focus on One, a teacher focuses on giving that one particular child special attention for a designated time, say one week, and observing any changes. The attention would include; eye contact, saying his/her name as you walk by, interaction, time, a touch on the shoulder - all the signals that say to the child, "I see you, I like you. You're special to me. We invite you into our space because you're one of us." This is a very non-threatening, non-invasive strategy that never forces reticent children to be in the limelight, but welcomes them on a personal, non-intrusive way. The Focus on One is usually very successful in bringing that child into active engagement with peers and learning situations.

Basic Skills Missed

Some English language learners missed acquiring certain phonetic skills important in literacy development. When students are learning English, they might not have the linguistic proficiency, at the time, to acquire a skill.

There could be language differences that interfered with learning English phonetics. Certain languages do not use consonant 'blends' as in gr, tr, pl, bl, st, etc., and so ELLs need practice listening for that 'second' consonant sound.

Also, certain English sounds do not occur in other languages.

ELLs learn the concept of rhyming words easily, as long as most of the words are in their English repertoire. But, some rhyming words are spelled differently, and that should be pointed out.
i.e., water - daughter

Learning vowel sounds are on the English Language Arts curriculum from grade 1 to grade 6, and for good reason.
ELLs may require review or remediation in learning;
- ✓ Short vowel sounds
- ✓ Silent letters
- ✓ Medial sounds
- ✓ Syllabication

Certain consonant varieties need to be highlighted, such as 'ch' in chef, Christine, chin.

Consonant Blends

Consonant blends are tricky for some language learners since it may not occur in their language.

Blended consonants are easy to learn, however, once the actual idea is shown and practised. When students know their blends, their spelling will improve. However some students may need help with their pronunciation.

Enunciate the blend sounds clearly and try to use words that students already know/understand.

'l' blends - bl   cl   fl   gl   pl   sl

'r' blends - br   cr   dr   fr   pr   tr

's' blends - st   sp   sm   sk   sn   sw   scr   squ

others - tw   qu

Digraphs
sh - ch - wh - th - qu - kn - ph - wr

To teach English language learners the special sounds of these, use words that are concrete &/ easy to draw. For example:

she, ship, shoe, sharp (knife/pencil), Shrek, shirt (tee-shirt), shadow, short, shoot

chips, China, chicken, chopsticks, children, checkmark, chin, cheap, cheese, chain

white, wheel, where, when, what, why, whale, whiskers, whip, whistle

th (careful - th has 2 sounds as in thin and that)
3 three, 30 thirty, Thursday, through (a tunnel), threw, thumb, thermometer

quiet, quarter, quit, question, squirrel (sounds like girl), quack, earthquake, queen

knife, knee, knock, know, tie a knot, knuckle
phone, photo/photograph, elephant, phlegm
write, wrestling, wrong, wrinkle, wrist, wrap up

Buddy Activities

The remaining section of this book provides a variety of 'buddy' activities; some are simple and work on primary skills while others are more difficult and challenging. Choose the activities you want to use for enrichment, skills development or review support.

Copy the activity on colored cardstock paper, and cover it with plastic or laminate. Office stores can do this as well.

Teachers may want to enlarge particular pages/activities before preparing the permanent activity card.

Certain activities list the number of sessions it would take to complete the task(s) properly.

Certain activities require particular materials.
i.e., choice of different bingo sets, sets of manipulative letters, atlases, science magazines, book sets, magazines

> A buddy leads a group through an activity.
> Talking is essential to the task.

The "What's Missing?" Game
For Beginners in English
Use School Items, Colored Markers, Plastic Animals,

> ➢ Take 6 objects to be learned.
>
> ➢ Hold up each one for students to see.
> ➢ Say the name clearly, and have students repeat it.
> ➢ Place the 6 items on the table. Point to each one and say the name again.
> ➢ Say, "Close your eyes". You might have to run your hand down over their eyes. Repeat "Close your eyes."
> ➢ Take and hide one of the objects in your lap.
> ➢ Say "Open your eyes."
> ➢ Whoever guesses the missing object first gets to hide the next object.
> ➢ You say, "Close your eyes."   "Open your eyes."
> ➢ Next, make it harder and take 2 or 3 objects.
> ➢ When the students know all the objects, start adding new ones. The game should be played several times.

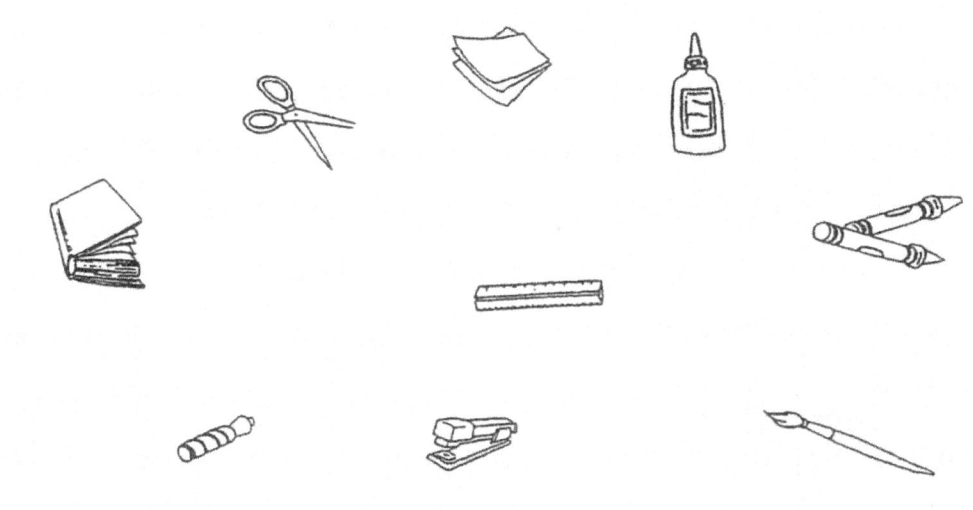

Mini-Books for Literacy

> Though language comes before Literacy,
> Literacy is always the goal.
>
> Language and Literacy ought to appear seamless;
> there's overlap and impetus to integrate speech with writing.
>
> Context extends comprehension; use examples in your lessons
> that students can relate to in their own lives and age group.

1. Use the book form for homework, buddy work or tutoring. Youngsters can draw a context; older students write and draw

2. Use the form for key words/terms of a topic. i.e., colors, family, field trip, as a book report to sequence a story or an experiment, a school week of weather, etc.

3. Enlarge the page for younger students who need a larger space for their drawings; their fine motor skills are not usually as well-developed as older students.

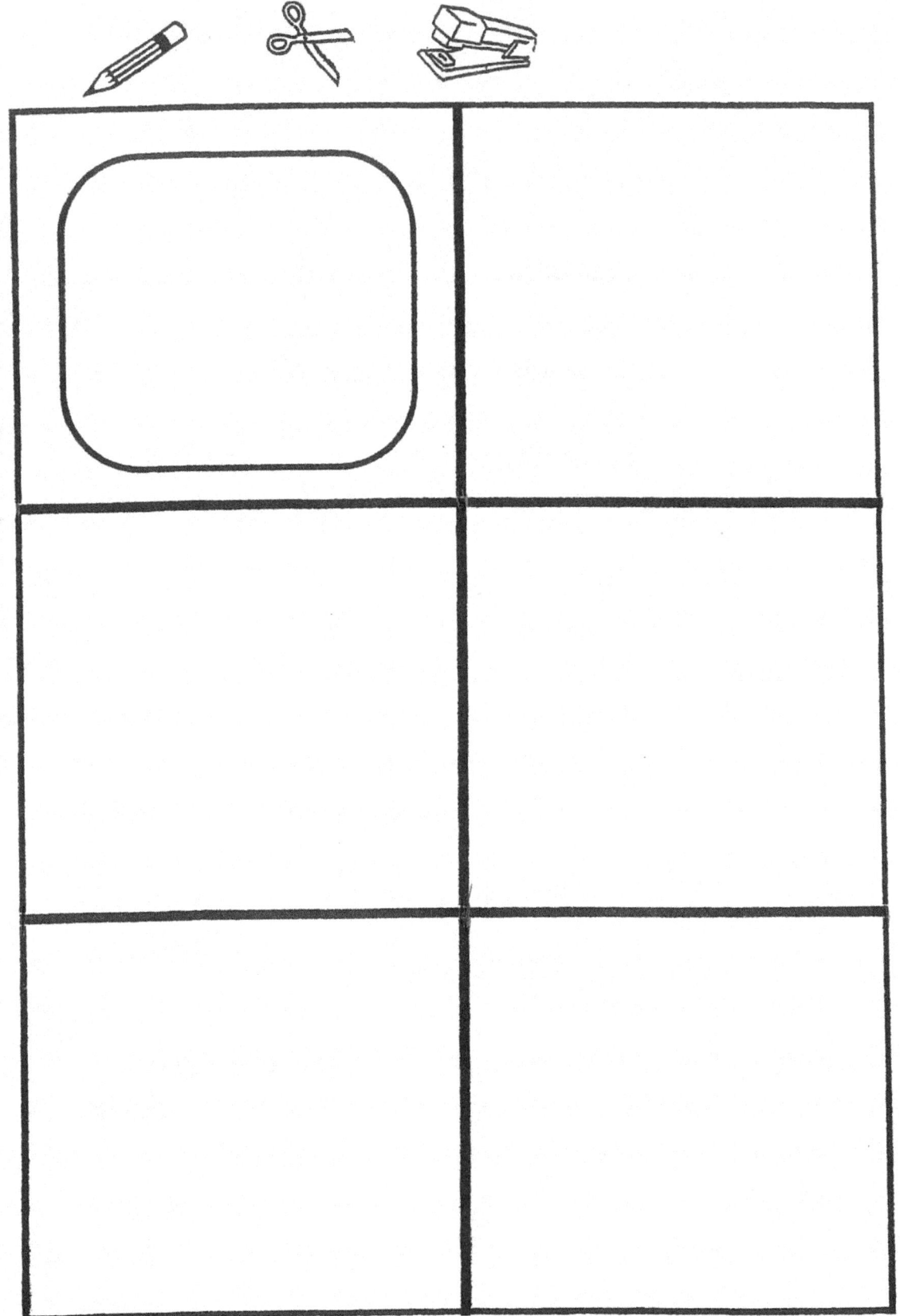

100s	10s	1s

My number is _____

Addition with Place Value Stamps

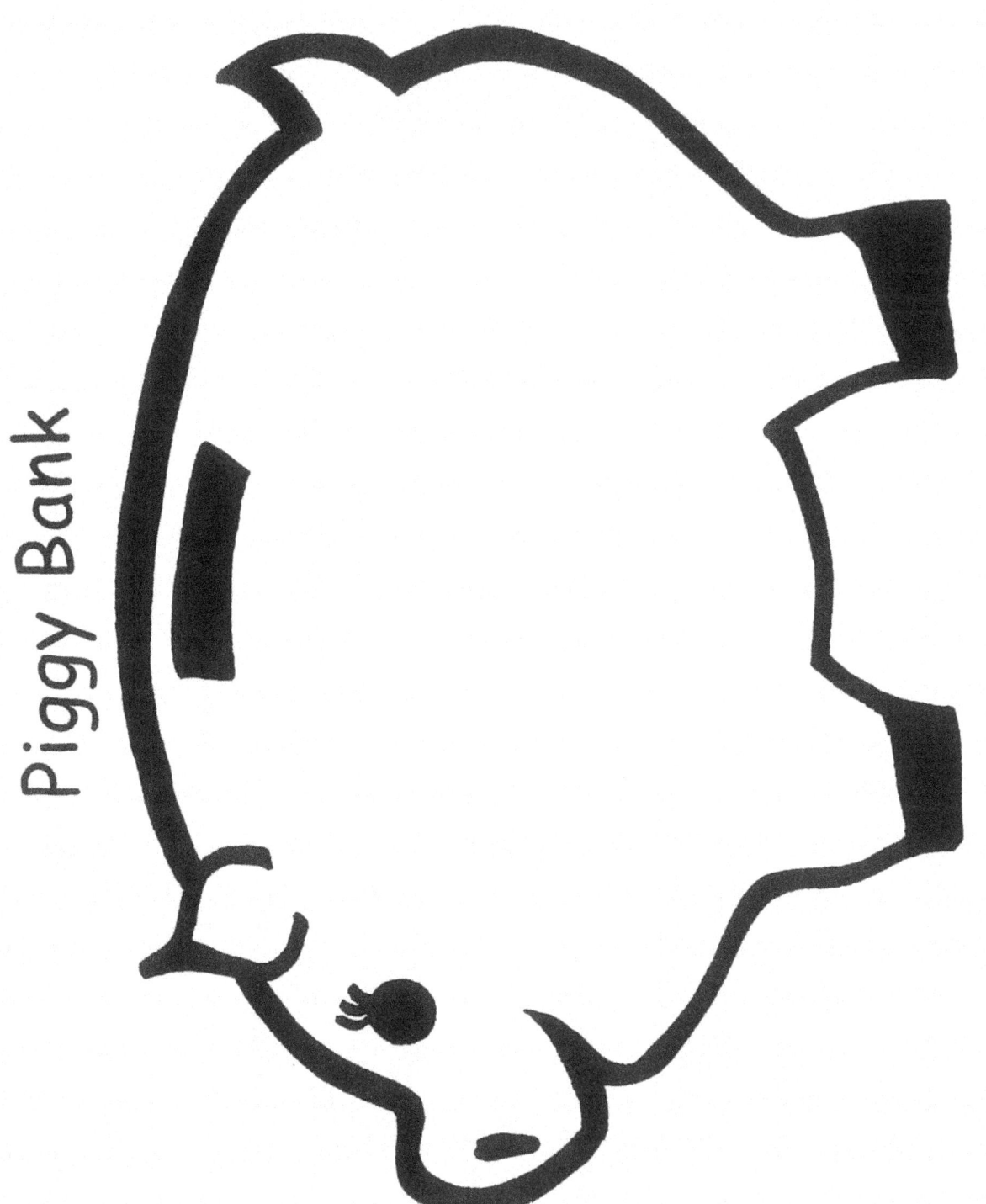

Piggy Bank

There is _____ in my piggy bank.

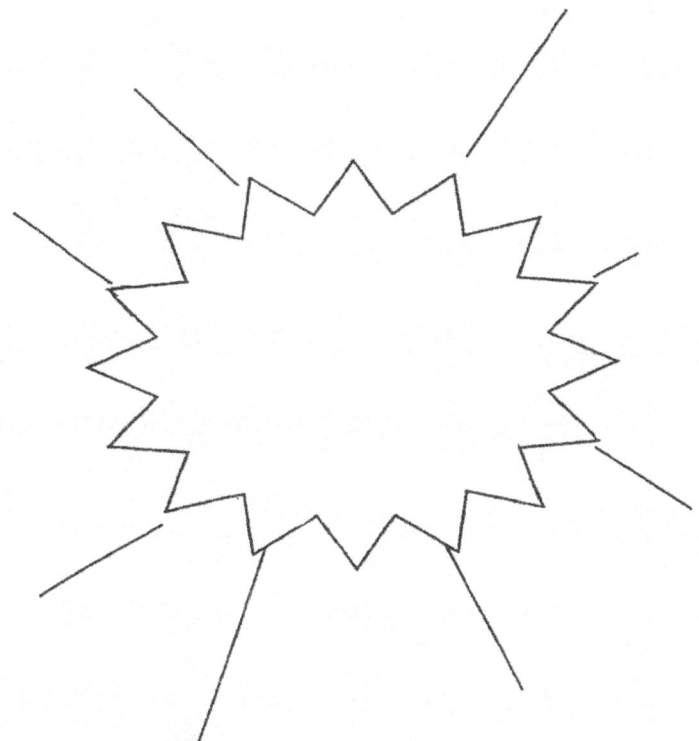

Topic Web

Internet Search

Ask and answer these questions. Q and A

Q. What is the difference between a frog and a toad?

A. _____

Q. What is the biggest toad?

A. _____

Q. What frog is poison?

A. _____

Q. How may eggs does a frog lay?

A. _____

Watch this video.

http://www.youtube.com/watch?v=oUBwBWC2oWQ

Help Students To Understand

This activity helps students to understand new work. The new work might be a story, a novel or a chapter, a worksheet or a book. Get the students to talk about what the questions mean, and then help with answers.

Content Title
Students write the name of what they are learning.

1. Key Vocabulary – means words important to the ideas
   * Ask students to find new and important words.
   * Ask students to write the words on the lines.

2. Help students to understand word meanings.
   * Let students translate, or try other ways to help.
   * When students understand the important words, they should say a short sentence for them.

3. A 'summary' tells important ideas in a paragraph or two. You don't know what the work is about so the students have to tell you.
   * Ask students what the story/work was all about.
   * Try and let everybody help summarize the ideas.
   * Make sure students put ideas in order.
   * Students write the summary when it makes sense.

4. Personal opinions – Talk about what they liked/disliked.

_____
Content Topic

1. Key Vocabulary

_____
_____
_____
_____
_____
_____

2. **Translate/use** the key words in sentences
3. **Summary** of the topic. Group Activity.

_____
_____
_____
_____
_____
_____
_____
_____

4. Personal responses or opinion.
_____
_____

Proper Nouns = Capitals for the Real Names

My name is _____

Write the Noun Person

1. your doctor's name _____

   your teacher's name _____

   your last name _____

Write the Noun Places

2. your address _____

   your city _____

   this country _____

Write the Noun Thing

3. your favorite TV show _____

   a food store _____

Proper nouns must have a capital letter.

Fooled You - 1 Session
Following Directions, Body Vocabulary

These are balancing tricks by Nancy Harvey.

Hopeless Hopper
Trick - There's no way students will be able to hop

First, ask the students to hop. Then tell them you will make it impossible for them to hop. Let 1 student try it first, and after that they can all try.
Tell the student to bend over and grab his toes. Gravity prevents them from hopping. They'll fall over.

Tiptoe Trap

Students will do this trick against a door, so make sure no one is coming in or going out. Hold the door so it doesn't bump into them. Ask students to stand up on their toes. Then choose 1 student to put their feet on either side of the door, with their stomach and nose touching the edge. Ask the student to stand on his/her toes. Then ask the student if his toes are glued to the floor.

Sticky Foot

You will stick the student's foot to the floor. Ask one student to stand sideways with one side of his body against the wall. Make sure that the student is touching the wall with his cheek, arm and foot. Then ask the student to lift up the other foot - the one farthest away from the wall. It will be impossible to do - because of balance.

State Your Opinion
How to say what you think or believe

1. Read these sentence starters that show you how to state an opinion.

a) <u>I think that</u> homework is a good idea.
b) <u>I believe that</u> homework is a good idea because . . . .
c) <u>In my opinion,</u> homework is not a good idea because . . . .
d) <u>It is my opinion that</u> kids need time for sports and play, and that. . .
e) <u>My opinion is that</u> parents and kids need to spend more time . . . . .

2. Think about your opinion about these things. Use the sentence starters.

    reading   pollution   cooking   aliens   computers

3. Express your opinions about 2 of those things with a partner.

4. Consider your opinion about a topic that interests you.
Write a paragraph to state your opinion. Then explain your opinion with reasons or examples. You have to say why you think that way.

Use the back of this paper.

        Pick a Topic _____
        Your Name _____

The A-B-C's of Countries

A_____   M_____

B_____   N_____

C_____   O_____

D_____   P_____

E_____   Q_____

F_____   R_____

G_____   S_____

H_____   T_____

I_____   U_____

J_____   V_____

K_____   W_____

L_____   X_____

Y_____

Z_____

Trick - If you get stuck, look in the Index.

Atlas and Map Activity – 2 Sessions
Understanding and Reading Maps

1. Get the tub of atlases.
2. Ask students to look through an atlas.
3. Encourage students to talk about what they find.
4. Ask students to go to the Table of Contents.
5. Show students that different country maps are on different pages.
6. Have students look for The World map page.
7. Have students find different countries.
8. Start the A-B-C's of Countries worksheet.

Thesaurus Activity – 1 Session
Understanding and Using a Thesaurus

1. Get the tub with all the thesauruses.
2. Ask students if they know what a "tyrannosaurus" is.
3. Tell them you have a tub of thesauruses, but they are not dinosaurs.
4. Give each student a thesaurus to look through.
5. Ask students what a dictionary is.
   (gives the definition/meaning/pronunciation)
6. Ask students to see what a Thesaurus does.
   (gives a choice of similar words to use)
7. Ask students to find the word "near" in the thesaurus.
8. Ask students how a thesaurus is organized. It is arranged in alphabetical order. Tell them if necessary.
9. Ask students to tell you the other words for "near".
10. Let each student think of an "adjective" for the other students to find. Read the alternatives.
11. Have students say a verb for others to find.

Country and Nationality

Country	Nationality
Canada	Canad<u>ian</u>
Italy	Italian
Iran	Iranian
Russia	Russian
Egypt	Egyptian
Mexico	Mexic<u>an</u>
Korea	Korean
America	American
Spain	Span<u>ish</u>
Ireland	Irish
England	English
China	Chin<u>ese</u>
Japan	Japanese
Vietnam	Vietnamese
France	French
Greece	Greek
Thailand	Thai

Look in an Atlas and say the names of other countries.

Find and draw things made of;
Translate these 5 words.

| wood |

| rubber |

| metal- steel |

| plastic |

Magnets

Magnets attract these.	Magnets repel these.

My magnet looks like this.

Categorize means to put things in groups, to sort things, to put things together that go together.

Here are some categories of			

wheels   music   places
water   people   plants
homes   vehicles   sports

Book Report

What is the name of your book?
The title is_____

Who is the author?
The author of the book is _____

Who is the illustrator?
The illustrator is_____

Who are the main characters?
The main characters are _____
_____

What is the plot?
What is the book about?
What happened in the story?
The book is about_____
_____
_____
_____
_____
_____

Summarize

Word: summarize (verb)
        summary (noun)

Definition:
to tell the main idea about what happened in a book, or a movie, or the news; to tell the important events

Example:
What was it about? Summarize it for me.

Important Vocabulary

main characters	sequence of events	genre
author	co-author	conclusion
setting	chapter	illustrator

Summary of _____

Name _____

Homonyms – 2 Words Sound the Same

Listen to the teacher's example sentences and translate unknown words.

rain - rein
write - right
our - hour
do - due
for - four
heel - heal
bored - board
close - clothes
break - brake
road - rode
led - lead
prints - prince
been - bean
waste - waist

stairs - stares
you're - your
there - their
steal - steel
oh - owe
tied - tide
side - sighed
some - sum
seen - scene
peace - piece
mail - male
know - no
hall - haul
roll – role

Write short sentences for 10 pairs of homonyms.

Words That Sound the Same – 2 Sessions
Understanding Different Meanings, Using Homonyms in Context

A) Read the pairs of words to the students. Then ask them if they can explain the difference between the words. If no one knows, show the meaning in a sentence.

B) Next, in partners students try to make a sentence.
For example: The knight left the castle at night. etc.

1 ad – add	2 choose – chews	3 ant – aunt
4 beat – beet	5 hi – high	6 die – dye
7 break – brake	8 mail – male	9 fair – fare
10 days – daze	11 higher – hire	12 fined – find
13 grown – groan	14 sent – cent	15 be – bee
16 led – lead	17 missed – mist	18 seize – sees
19 night – knight	20 Maine – main	21 not – knot
22 side – sighed	23 pain – pane	24 rose – rows
25 rough – ruff	26 pail – pale	27 oh – owe
28 horse – hoarse	29 or – oar	30 flu – flew
31 aloud – allowed	32 creek – creak	33 hey – hay
34 four – for	35 fairy – ferry	36 dear – deer
37 guessed – guest	38 flea – flee	39 hall – haul
40 heard – herd	41 I'll – aisle	42 we'd – weed
43 beat – beet	44 do – due	45 red – read

46 presents – presence

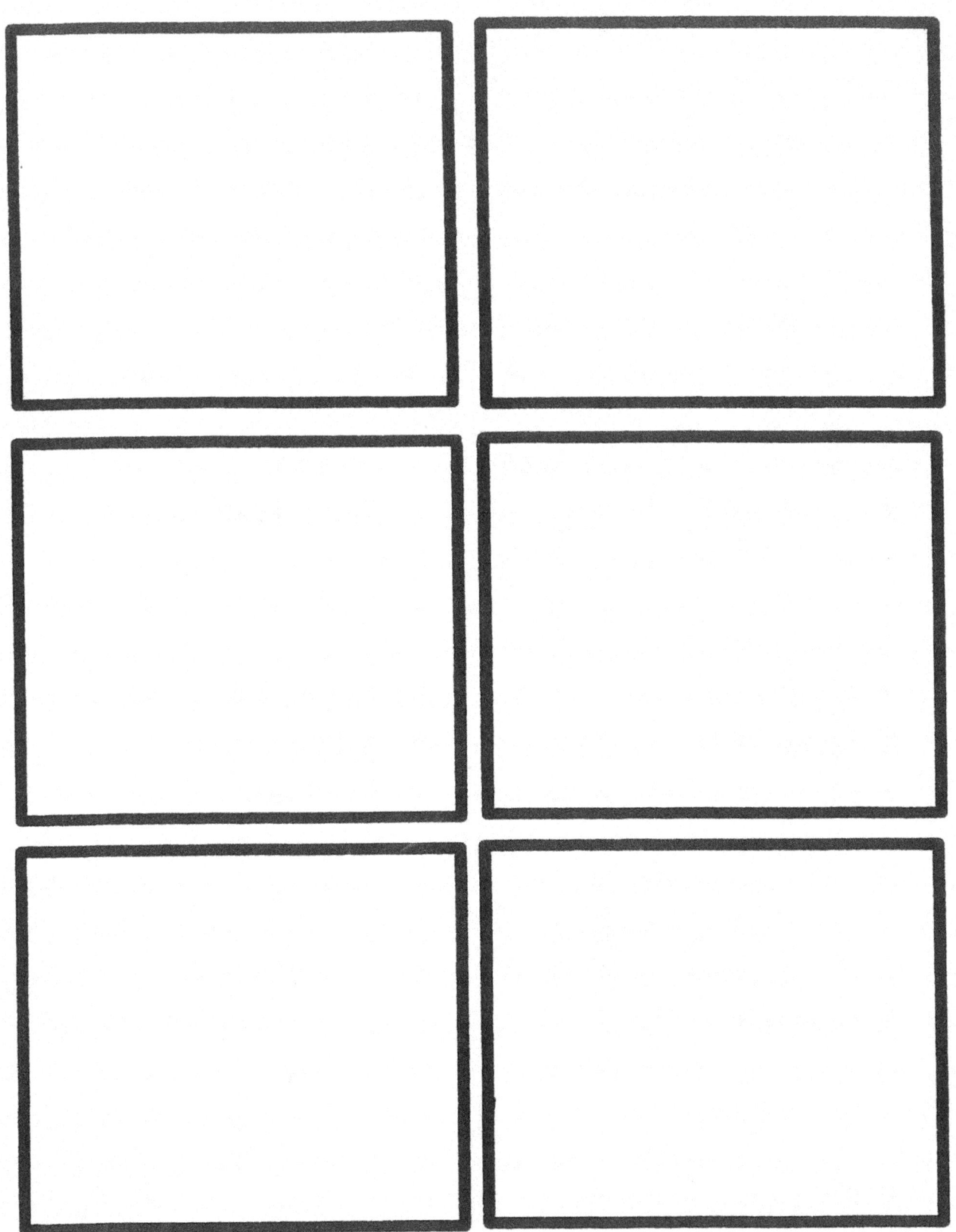

Copy twice and make a matching card game.

They sound the same.

-er   -ur   -ir

1. Listen to the teacher read these words. Circle -er.

   her   helper   better   teacher   faster

---

2. Listen to the teacher read these words. Circle -ur.

   turn   burn   burp   slurp   hurt   fur

---

3. Listen to the teacher read these words. Circle -ir.

   girl   dirt   sir   bird   shirt

---

a) Write each word on the back of this paper.

b) Get a partner. You say one of the words and your partner must say if it is spelled with -er, -ur   -ir.

Rain, rain go away
Come again another day

(ai) makes the same sound as (ay)

1. Read these 'ai' words.
   rain   pail   afraid   first aid

2. Make rhyming words.
   tail   f____   m____
   rain   p____   st____

3. Read these 'ay' words
   stay   pray   clay   today
   away   lay   tray   maybe

4. Make rhyming words.
   day _____   _____   _____   _____

5. Use the right word.
   a)   He's hurt. He needs first _____.
   b)   My sister is _____ of deep water.
   c)   I can't go out _____. I have to _____ home.
   d)   I have to study so I won't _____ the test.
   e)   Some dogs have their _____ cut off.
   f)   Don't do that _____.
   g)   _____ down and go to sleep.

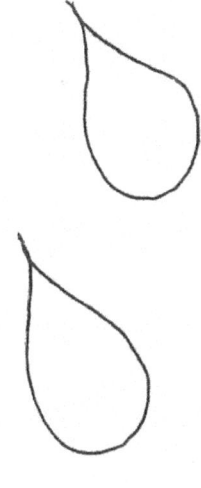

Rain rain
Go away
Come again
Some other day

ai makes the same sound as **ay**.

1. Read these words and underline the **ai**.

rain   pain   again   stain

afraid   paid   first aid

tail   fail   mail   jail

2. Write the correct word in these sentences.

It's going to _____ so get an umbrella.
He's _____ of the teacher.
He went to the doctor because of the _____.
When a dog wags its _____, that means its friendly.
Study so you won't _____.
Don't do that _____.
Get the _____ _____ kit. He cut himself.
_____ is for bad guys.

A Paragraph

Translate the word paragraph.

Definition
A paragraph is a group of sentences about the same idea.
There are usually 4 or more sentences in a paragraph.

Sometimes the first line of a paragraph is indented.
On a computer, the 'Tab' key indents.

Also, there is often a line space before a new paragraph.

Do This

1. Write a paragraph about computers.

2. Write a paragraph about your favorite TV show.

3. Write a paragraph about your best friend.

Topic Paragraphs

1. Write a paragraph about your favorite movie.

2. Write a paragraph about a friend.

3. Write a paragraph about 1 million dollars.

4. Write a paragraph about your family.

5. Write a paragraph about music.

6. Write a paragraph about yourself.

7. Write a paragraph about your future.

8. Write a paragraph about bullies.

9. Write a paragraph about sports.

10. Write a paragraph about school.

Emotions are Feelings

In stories and in movies,
the events happen because of
someone's feelings or emotions.

Go to this Internet website and make your own list of words that describe emotions. List some emotion words and translate them.

www.english-at-home.com
/vocabulary/english-word-for-emotions

___ ___ ___ ___

___ ___ ___ ___

___ ___ ___ ___

Research Activity - 4 Sessions
Locating and Using a Different Information Sources

Session # 1
1. Go to the library with your group. They must bring their pencils and workbooks.
2. Sit them down, and ask students to tell you what kinds of books are in the library.
3. Help them to make a list the different kinds of books; story books. For example, true stories (non-fiction) and made up stories (fiction) stories about famous people (biographies) etc.
4. Walk your students around the library in single file to look at, and name the kinds of books on the shelves.
5. Find out where the magazine collections are.
6. If there is time they can look at the magazines.

Research Activity - 4 Sessions
Locating and Using a Different Information Sources

Session # 2
1. Go back to the library with your group and sit down.
2. Remind them of the walk around that they did before. Help them to add more kinds of books to their list.
3. Tell the students that a man, Mr. Dewey organized all the different topics of books by numbering them.
4. Then, single file, walk the group around to identify the kinds of books in the Dewey Decimal System.
- Name the categories of books in the 1 to 100 numbers
- 100 to 200 books in the Dewey system
- 200 to 300 books etc. to the end
5. If you have time, show students where to find the different encyclopedias and the World Books.

Research Activity - 4 Sessions
Locating and Using a Different Information Sources

Session # 3
1. Go back to the library with your group and sit down.
2. Remind them of the walk around that they did before. Help them to add more kinds of books to their list.
3. Tell the students that before computers, people used encyclopedias for research.
4. Walk the group to the encyclopedias and identify the names of several sets. Ask students to see how they are organized. (alphabet and/or number)
5. Point out and identify other kinds of books. For example, the maps and atlas section.
6. Have students add them to their list of books.
7. Locate shelves with book series.
8. Let students read until it is time to go.

Research Activity - 4 Sessions
Locating Books Using the Computer and Dewey System

Session # 4
1. Go back to the library with your group and sit down.
2. Ask the students if they remember the Dewey system.
3. Go to the library computer for locating books.
4. Show students how to use the search method by author, subject or title.
5. Ask each student to tell you something they are interested in, and to print it in the subject section.
6. Then, tell the student to find the Dewey section, and bring back a book to show you.
7. Ask students to use the computer to locate other topics.
8. Take several students with you to return the books in the correct place.

Count Dracula Counts

Students staple 11 pages together, cut and paste and draw matching pictures.

1 castle is where I live.

2 cats sleep in my coffin.

3 pumpkins are at my door.

4 eyeballs are in my lunch.

5 masks hide my friends.

6 ghosts make music for me.

7 skeletons dance in the wind.

8 old doors are up the stairs.

 9 drops of blood

are in my juice.

10 gravestones are in my yard.

Compound Words - 2 words in 1

Read then say these words. Draw a line between the two words.

it/self
newspaper
suitcase
schoolyard
stepmother
bullfighter
campground
suntan
earthworm
breakfast
forget
thunderstorm
headquarters
ponytail

airlines
handout
skateboarding
greenhouse
legroom
underdog
championship
cheerleader
snowflake
blueberries
motorcycle
firecrackers
thoughtless
girlfriend

earrings
outside
cupboard
uptight
sunrise
toothpaste
volleyball
windsurf
leadership
jellyfish
thunderbolt
outline
crosswalk
pickpocket

Seasons

Translate the words Summer, Fall or Autumn, Winter, Spring

Draw symbols for the weather, special days and activities in each season.

Look at an Atlas world map. Identify the Equator, North and South Poles

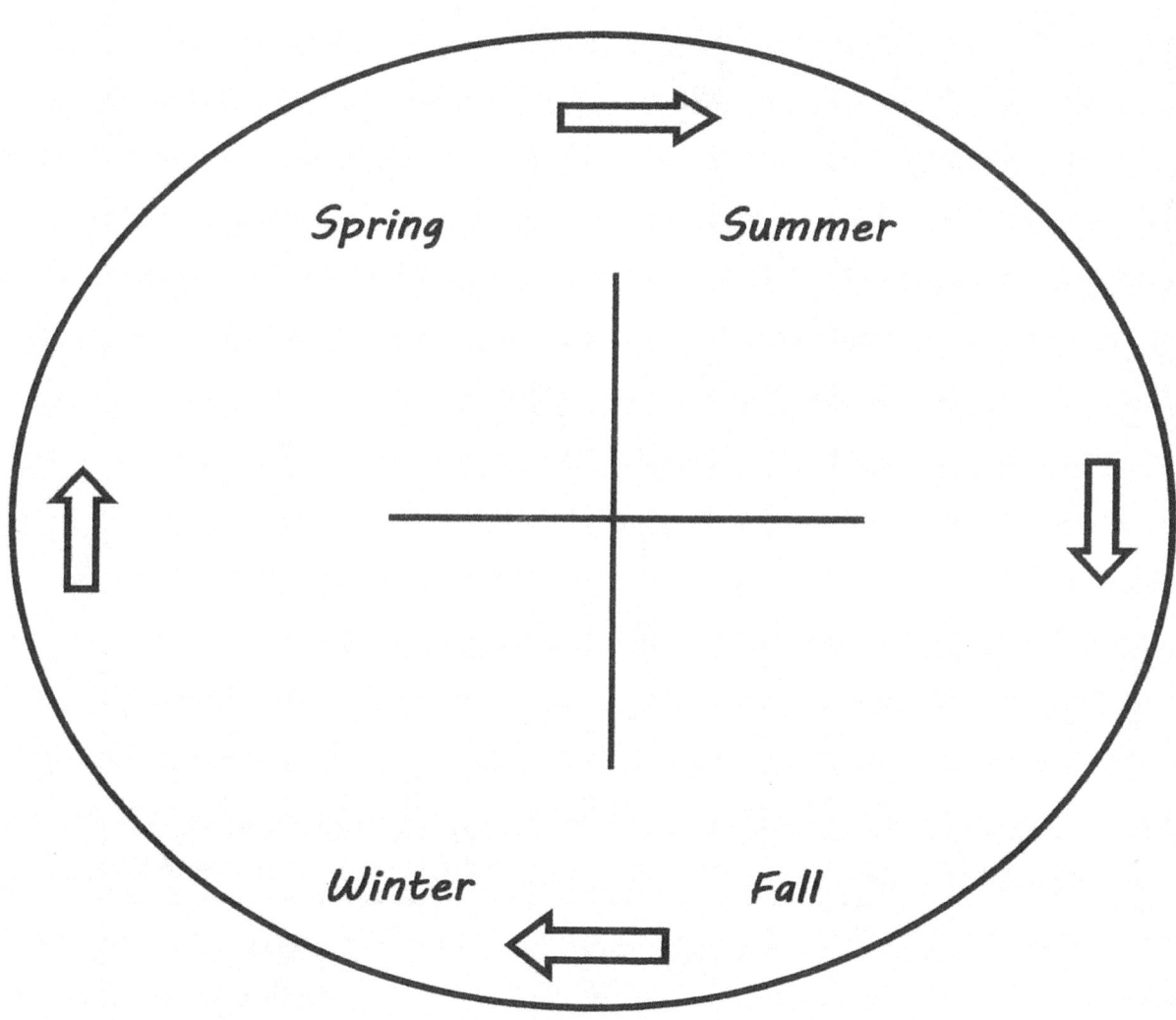

Get Dressed!

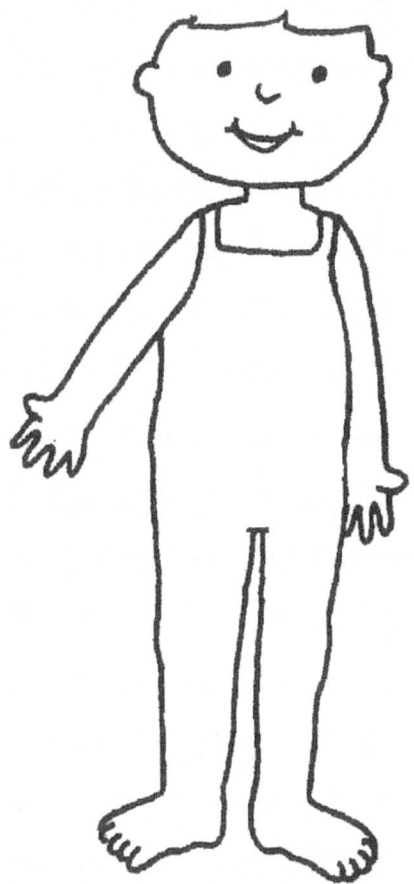

Draw the face and hair of a girl or a boy.
Roll the dice, name the matching clothes and draw it on the body.
Roll the same number, and you're out of luck. The winner finishes first.

1. underwear   2. jeans   3. socks

4. shoes    5. tee-shirt   6. jacket

Winter Activities

Roll the dice, call the words and draw the items on the paper.
Roll the same number, and you're out of luck. The winner finishes first.

1. hills of snow	2. trees	3. an ice rink
4. skiers and snowboarders	5. skaters	6. people tobogganing

What's in MY Bag?
Forming Questions

1. Get a medium size bag that students cannot see through.
2. Put an object from a unit of study, into the bag.
3. Hold up the bag and say, "What's in my bag?"
4. Tell students to guess (new word) the object.
   Note if students can form a question or a yes/no question.
5. If students are not getting close to the answer, then give a riddle/hint (new words). Use size, color, use, material
6. Also let one student feel the object outside the bag. If that doesn't work, let a student put a hand in the bag to feel the object.

Objects in the bag
- a plant for spring - a toy seal for an animal unit
- an artifact/ microscope/ ruler/mitten, etc

Pronouns
Replace a Noun

That's _____ book.
That's _____ book.
That's _____ book.
That's _____ book.
That's _____ book.
Those are _____ books.
Those are _____ books.

Please give it to _____ .
Please give it to _____ .
Please give it to _____ .
Please give it to _____ .

I can do it _____ .
He can do it _____ .
She can do it _____ .
You can do it _____ .
We can do it _____ .
They can do it _____ .

Writing Know How
Function - Suggesting, Advising

Words to use.
Read the words.
Listen to your teacher's examples.

You should . . .   Why don't you . . .   I'd suggest that . . .

I think you . . .   You ought to . . .   You'd better . . .

My advice would be . . .   It would be a good idea . . .

Write a suggestion, or give advice for each problem below.

1. your big brother smokes too much
2. your friend has a bad cold
3. your mother works too much
4. two little kids are fighting
5. your sister has a math test tomorrow
6. lots of students are shouting in the class
7. a kid's crayon has rolled far under the couch
10. it's 1 o'clock in the morning, and your mom is still reading
11. somebody is playing with matches
12. the baby is crying

Helping Verbs

Examples - do, did, does, may might, should, would, could, was, were, can, have, has, had, must, ought, shall, used to

Circle the helping verbs in these sentences.

1. He ought to study before 10 o'clock, or he may fall asleep.
2. I shall give more money to poor people.
3. He has to stop his homework now.
4. She ought to win first prize for her story.
5. I can do the homework later tonight.
6. The dog has chewed all my shoes.
7. You should stretch first or you could get sore muscles.
8. Did you get the marks back from your test?
9. He used to ski.
10. You did not try hard enough.
11. I could swim across that lake.
12. Could I borrow some money?
13. It might rain tomorrow. I might stay home.
14. Don't count on me for a ride. I might be too busy.
15. Shall I help you with those bags?
16. My friend said that he would help me.
17. There used to be an office over there.
18. Everybody must obey the law.

Future Tense Verbs

I will = a promise

I'm going to = a plan

I might = a possibility

1. What have you promised your mom?

I will _____

I will _____

I will _____

2. What are you doing this weekend?

I'm going to/ I'm gunna _____

I'm going to _____

I'm going to _____

3. What are you going to do when you are an adult?

I might _____

I might _____

I might _____

Will Not = Won't

Change the verb 'will not' to won't in these sentences.

1. He will not help me.
   He _____ help me.

2. I will not finish this much pizza.
   I _____ finish this much pizza.

3. She will not have enough money to go out.
   She _____ have enough money to go out.

4. There will not be a test tomorrow.
   There _____ be a test tomorrow.

5. He will not go to horror movies.
   He _____ go to horror movies.

6. My mom will not let me go with you.
   My mom _____ let me go with you.

7. The TV will not work.
   The TV _____ work.

8. She will not be able to come to my birthday party.
   She _____ be able to come to my birthday party.

Fill in the boxes with the correct verbs.

Past	Present	Future
Sold		will sell
	tell	
	sing	
	speak	
	get	
	read	
	say	

My name is _____

Idioms – 2 Sessions

A. Listen as each sentence is spoken.
B. Guess the meanings.
C. Write the real meaning beside each idiom.
D. Draw a picture about one of the idioms on another paper.
E. Write the idiom on the back of the drawing.
F. Staple the idiom pictures into a booklet.

1. Take it easy.
2. I'm broke.
3. He lost his temper.
4. We don't see eye to eye.
5. The baby cried his eyes out.
6. You're driving me up a wall.
7. You must be nuts!
8. Take my word for it.
9. Quit beefing!
10. Keep an eye out.
11. You're pulling my leg.
12. It's raining cats and dogs.
13. She broke my heart.
14. Stop monkeying around.
15. Over my dead body.
16. Don't cry over spilt milk.
17. Don't put all your eggs in one basket.
18. Take a load off your feet.
19. Easy come, easy go.
20. He cracks me up.
21. He's crying his head off.
22. Give me a break, will you?
23. He's on cloud nine.
24. He's all butterfingers.
25. I have butterflies in my stomach.
26. Money burns a hole in my pocket.
27. That movie gave me goose bumps.
28. I'm feeling blue.

Fortune Teller Square
Using the Future Tense

TEACHER, PLEASE ENLARGE COPIES OF THE SQUARE.
Fold in half A to B. Open. Fold in half again top to bottom. Open again. Fold all 4 corners into the middle and press. Turn the paper over. Fold the corners in the center again. Fold the top to the bottom. Fold one side to the other.

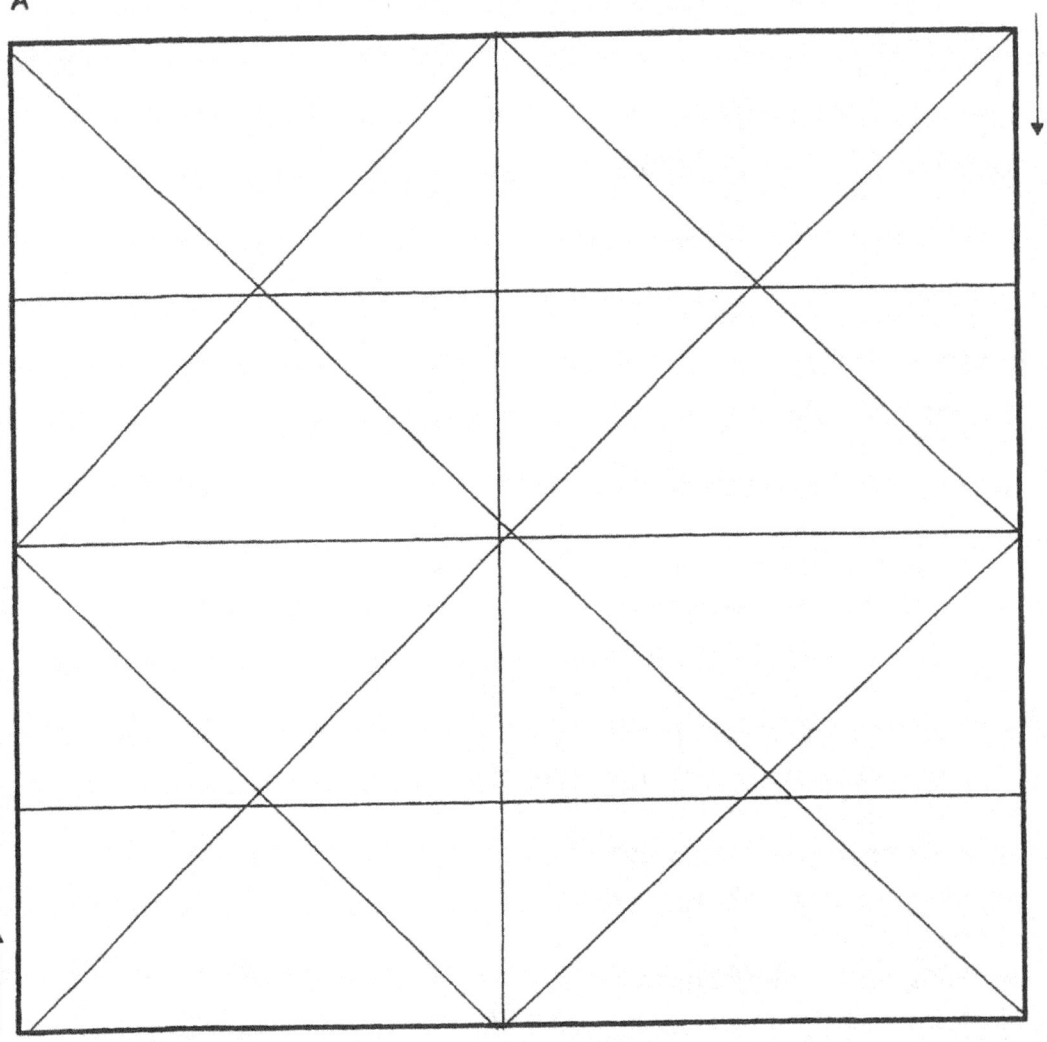

Fortune Teller
Using the Future Tense

1. Every student takes one of the play papers and a pencil.
2. Fold the paper in half. Crease it. Then fold it in half again, and press /crease along the fold.
3. Show the students step by step how to finish the folds.
4. On the outer spaces, students choose to write either a color or a student's name (8 spaces).
5. On the inner flaps, students write a number.
6. On the inside spaces, students must write a fortune such as - You will take a trip to Japan.
   You will have 3 children.
   You will become famous.
   You will marry a genius. Etc.
7. When the games are finished, let the students play it in the group.

Mad Libs Books - 1 Session
Parts of Speech

1. Show one of the Mad Lib books to the group. Explain how you make the story by adding parts of speech.
2. Do an example of one of the stories with the group.
3. Allow the students to work in partners to complete several stories.
4. Have the students read their story to the whole group.

What's My Job? - 2 Sessions
Verbs, Occupations Vocabulary

1. Students listen as you read the rows of job names.
2. When you finish each row ask students if they know what each person does. Some students might need a translation or explanation of the meaning.

Row 1	Row 2	Row 3
actor	doctor	driver
hairstylist	dentist	singer
pilot	lawyer	nurse
mail carrier	secretary	baker
musician	writer	artist
chef	programmer	courier
caretaker	accountant	electrician
teacher	pharmacist	salesclerk
animator	butcher	plumber
scientist	journalist	police
model	soldier	producer
veterinarian	magician	cashier
director	athlete	barber
designer	paramedic	farmer
forest ranger	carpenter	builder
detective	church leader	coroner
security guard	T.V. Announcer	surgeon

3. Play Password with each row. In this game, a player says a word connected with a job and everyone has to guess the answer. Whoever guesses gets one point.
   for example; trees - forest ranger
4. In the second session, read the words again by row, and show students how to mark stress. For example; detective
5. Play password again.

Computer Words and Commands

1. computer   on   off   Programs   plugin   Modem   Printer   Ink Cartridge

2. e-mail address   Sign in   Password   Hotmail   Rogers   Yahoo   Junk   Delete

3. keyboard   keys   type   arrow keys   Caps lock   screen   monitor

4. mouse   cursor   move it around   click   control

5. Internet   website   Search   Keywords   View   Bookmark this site

6. erase   Delete   the Undo key   the Redo key   gone   lost

7. word program   write   save   save as title   file name   location

8. space   backspace

9. Menu bar   dropdown menu

10. edit   fix   cut and paste   copy and paste   Tools help

11. scroll across   Hold cursor down and scroll across

12. Font   "What font do you like?"   Change fonts   bold   letters   Italics

13. File   Where you save your work - name the file - location

14. size   Font size   Line spacing   Page size   Change page size

15. Capital   shift down   - to make signs above numbers

16. Spellcheck   replace   skip   close   Dictionary   Thesaurus   Grammar check

17. Printer   Print   Color   All   Range   Pages   Cancel

18. hyphen   dash   numbers   @ # $ % & * ( ) +

19. audio   turn up   turn down

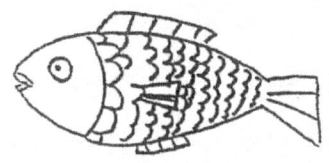

English Food Words

Session 1
Making Food Cards

Use grocery flyers to make a variety of cut and paste picture cards. Tell students we cannot have 2 of the same item. Encourage students to find pictures for all the Food Groups. Collect the cards, show each one and say the name of the item. Students repeat the words.

Session 2
Learning the Names of Food

First, the teacher will say the name of each food card. Pronounce each item slowly, and stress each syllable. Then say the word at normal speed. Students should repeat the words. Ask for translations in their language.

Give each student 2 large circles. Make one circle have a happy mouth, and the second circle have a sad mouth. Students tape or glue the heads on each side of a flat stick or ruler. Show the happy face and say," I like." Show the sad face and say, "I don't like." Translate these.

Finally, teachers hold up a food card and say its name. Students must show their happy face if they like it, or sad face if they don't like the food.

English Food Words

Session 3
Understanding Food Groups
Prepare 5 paper bags with a different food group picture.
1. Milk Group, 2. Cereals, Bread, Pasta, Rice, 3. Meat, Fish Poultry, Nuts, 4. Fruit and Vegetables, 5. Snacks
Repeat the names of each food. Have students take turns to name a picture and put it in the right Food Group bag.

Session 4
The Shopping Game
Shuffle the food cards and turn them face down. One student turns over a card, names it and adds it to his/her own shopping bag (plastic/paper). The first student to get 10 different food cards in his/her shopping bag is the winner. Play several times.

Session 5
The Dinner Game
Each student uses one plate either paper or Styrofoam. Explain that students will make their dinner. Translate. Students turn over a card, say it, and put it on his/her plate. The winning student gets five correct food items first. Tell students; no coffee, no chocolate bars, candy or chips at dinner. Water is good, but not cans of pop.

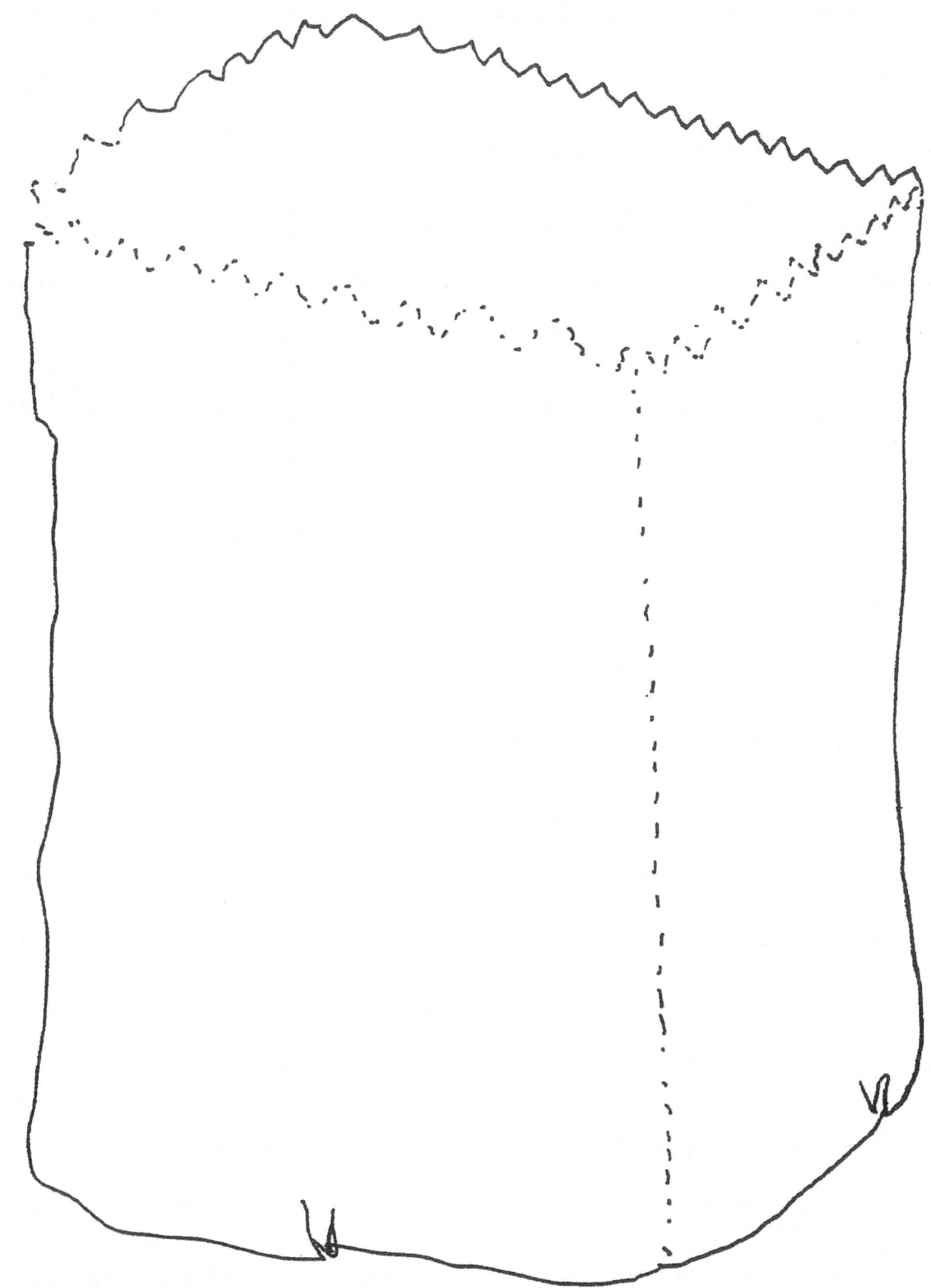

Cut and paste food pictures from store flyers.

Alphabet Activities

Alphabet Books - 3 Sessions
Students Create an Alphabet Book

1. Show students all different kinds of Alphabet Books.
2. Let the students look at the books and talk about the different kinds.
3. Read a couple of different examples.
4. Have students choose a style they like and then they create their own alphabet book.
5. Help with spelling and ideas.

Alphabet Fonts - 2 Sessions
Learning the Alphabet and Sequencing. Learning computer fonts.

1. Each student is given a paper with the alphabet.
2. Students must write the alphabet on the computer. Check that the sequence is correct.
3. Show students how to copy and paste new alphabets.
4. Then, show students how to scroll over one set, go up to Font to change the style. Create 6 sets.
5. Finally, students print out their work.

Alphabet Phonics - 4 Sessions
Learning Letter Sounds

1. Each student is given clay or plasticene.
2. They are to make a small object that starts with a letter of the alphabet. Help them with shape and details. They will keep all the objects in a shoebox.
3. When they are finished, show the rest of the class.

Manipulative Alphabet Letters

Use the following manipulative letters:
- ✓ To sequence the alphabet
- ✓ To practice spelling words
- ✓ To review key vocabulary
- ✓ To form and sequence grade one reading vocabulary

Make multiple copies of the alphabet letters on different colours of stock card, which lasts longer than if you use construction paper. If there is no facility to do this in your school board, then go to a business store. These hand made letter sets are much cheaper than commercial sets, and easier to replace when some get lost.

A	B	C
G	H	I
M	N	O

D	E	F
J	K	L
P	Q	R

S	T	U
Y	Z	a
e	f	g

V	W	X
b	c	d
h	i	j

k	l	m
q	r	s
w	x	y

In-School Activities
Language Improvement Clubs

- Last Class Period
- After School Club

- Board Games
- Book and Magazine Club
- Reading Club (self initiated, varied genre)
- Writing Club
- Technology Club
- Arts and Crafts
- Student Culture Newsletter
- Outdoor Education/ Science/ Nature
- Computer Club
- Homework Club
- Cooking Club
- Language Buddies Tutoring Club
- _____